In Pursuit of *Mr. Right*

By

Pastor Ira J. Acree

In Pursuit of Mr. Right
Copyright © 2011 by: Ira J. Acree

ISBN-13: 978-0-9831317-9-3
ISBN-10: 0983131791

All rights reserved solely by the author. The author certifies all contents are original and do not infringe upon the legal rights of any other person or work. No part of this book may be reproduced in any form without the permission of the publisher. The views expressed in this book are not necessarily those of the publisher.

Unless otherwise indicated, all scriptural references are taken from the New International Version®, NIV®. Copyright © 1973, 1978, 1984, 2011 by Biblica, Inc.™ Used by permission of Zondervan. All rights reserved worldwide www.zondervan.com.

Passages marked (KJV) are taken from the Authorized King James Version

Printed in the United States
10 9 8 7 6 5 4 3 2 1

Cover design and interior layout by:
Latoya Bady,
TBady Graphic Designs
Chicago Illinois
Tbady@live.com

Literary consultation services provided by:
Dr. Dennis J. Woods
Life To Legacy, LLC
P.O. Box 1239
Matteson, IL 60443
(877) 267-7477

Presented to:

To contact the author
go to
Info@gsjbchurch.org

Table of Contents

Introduction..i

Chapter 1
Trapped by Tradition..................................1

Chapter 2
It's Alright to Make the First Move............7

Chapter 3
Who's Zoomin' Who?................................11

Chapter 4
The Queen of Sheba.................................19

Chapter 5
Never Abandon Your Support System......25

Chapter 6
The Value of a Good Reputation...............31

Chapter 7
Confirm His Wealth...................................37

Chapter 8
Ladies Save Your Spices!..........................49

Chapter 9
Final Words...57

Introduction

Today in America, with all of the achievements that Black women have made in cracking the proverbial glass ceiling, there still seems to be one important area of their lives that remains quite elusive. No matter how much they have accomplished in business, or how high they have risen in academia, or what level of social status they have attained, despite all their achievements, in terms of relationships, many women are still very unmarried.

Though they drive expensive cars and live in posh dwelling places, women are finding it rather challenging living alone way up there in "stellar" heights. However, not only are the upwardly mobile climbing-the-corporate-ladder sisters experiencing a lack of meaningful relationships with men, but our churches are also full of women who don't seem to understand what's really going on with finding and keeping a good man.

Ironically, for the Christian woman, much of the problem is what they have been taught in church. By trying to make one scripture fit all circumstances, countless women have missed the 'real deal' on how the happily-ever-after hook-up really happens.

As a pastor, I hear all the stories and get all the complaints from women about how there's no good men out there. They say that the men that are out there aren't worthy of them. I even hear that when they do find a prospective man who starts out being interesting and interested, he turns out to be another deadbeat once his real issues start to surface. Therefore, many women throw up their hands and throw in the towel, and in the process become either callous or hopeless.

In order to shed some light on this issue, we can't go to Internet chat rooms, or social networking sites, or television talk shows, but we need to seek answers and wisdom from the Word of God. Therefore, let's turn to 1 Kings chapter 10, verses 1-7.

> When the queen of Sheba heard about the fame of Solomon and his relation to the name of the LORD, she came to test

him with hard questions. Arriving at Jerusalem with a very great caravan—with camels carrying spices, large quantities of gold, and precious stones—she came to Solomon and talked with him about all that she had on her mind. Solomon answered all her questions; nothing was too hard for the king to explain to her. When the queen of Sheba saw all the wisdom of Solomon and the palace he had built, the food on his table, the seating of his officials, the attending servants in their robes, his cupbearers, and the burnt offerings he made at the temple of the LORD, she was overwhelmed. She said to the king, "The report I heard in my own country about your achievements and your wisdom is true. But I did not believe these things until I came and saw with my own eyes. Indeed, not even half was told me; in wisdom and wealth you have far exceeded the report I heard.

I want to talk about being "In Pursuit of Mr. Right."

At Greater St. John Bible Church of Chicago, where I pastor, during the latter part of 2011, I taught a challenging series on marital relationships from both the male and the female perspectives. However, during the last part of that series, I focused more attention on women's issues in marriage and relationships. I was upfront with everyone and candidly explained that I wouldn't be talking about the birds and the bees, or storks delivering babies—none of that folklore stuff. I wanted to conduct a real "rubber-meets-the-road" discussion about all of the serious issues that surround the topic of intimate relationships between men and women.

Chapter 1

TRAPPED BY TRADITION

"Never allow outdated and unbiblical traditions govern nor dictate your life. It could cause you to miss out on significant blessings."

As I have learned from my own personal experiences and from counseling countless individuals and couples over the years, there are several barriers that obstruct establishing and maintaining meaningful relationships. Some of those barriers are the very concepts that we hold so dear when it comes to how we think about the opposite sex. As I just stated, storks don't bring babies, but men and women having sexual intercourse does. I state the obvious to make an important point. It's ideas like storks and birds and bees that allows us to evade reality and the real issues concerning the natural attraction to the opposite sex.

Young ladies, let me be very candid with you. It's not abnormal, dysfunctional, or even sinful when you desire to have a man. You do not have to retreat to denial or magical thinking. You do not have to be down on yourself. And you certainly do not have to let anyone else make you feel like you are "thirsty" or desperate because you are interested in pursuing a man of your liking. It's natural to be interested in a man. It's natural to have an inclination for a man, as long as you do not go overboard and start stalking the man. Listen, as slim as the pickings are for good men these days, if he is your Mr. Right, you better know how to pursue him, and if you catch him, you better know how to keep him. You must also realize that slim picking means that the competition is fierce from sister-girl next door.

The situation being what it is, now requires a revolutionary response, women now have to pursue the man. I know, this concept completely shatters the traditional relationship mold. I also know that this may cut against "the religious grain" and buck some biblical tradition that teaches us that the only one who is to do the pursuing is the man. Therefore, I know there may be some old-schoolers reading this book and asking, "Where did he get this from?"

First off, let me acknowledge that Proverbs 18:22 does say, "he that finds a wife finds a good thing," there is no disputing that. However, there are some historical/cultural things to consider back then, about three or so thousand years ago. Back then, you had a male dominated culture, even much more than you do today. If a man liked a woman, he would ask the father for her, and they'd cut the deal. If she were lucky, the prospective wife would find out about this deal *before* the wedding day. If the father liked the man (never mind the prospective wife at this point) and said okay, the prospective husband would pay the father for her. The bride's price was called a dowry. Try that one today!

After this transaction, the couple could get married. But sometimes you could end up getting a raw deal, especially if the husband to be was dealing with a *slick* daddy, like in Jacob's case. For example, in Genesis 29, we have the story of how Laban, the uncle of Jacob, pulled a bait and switch move on his nephew Jacob. Jacob wanted to marry Laban's daughter Rachel. As it was their custom, Jacob had to pay his uncle for Rachel's hand in marriage. Since Jacob didn't have money, he agreed to work for his uncle for seven years in order to marry Rachel.

After the seven years was up, Jacob finally married Rachel. On that long anticipated wedding day, that night was full of romance. Back then when the husband and wife came together the marriage was officially consummated. However, when the next morning came, Jacob rolled over to behold his beautiful new bride only to find out it wasn't Rachel, it was her older sister Leah! Old slickster Laban, under the cover of night, switched daughters on Jacob.

Jacob, obviously besides himself, confronted Laban, who explained that it was against their custom for the younger daughter to be given away in marriage before the older daughter. So in order to marry Rachel now, Jacob had to agree to work for his uncle *another* seven years! Talking about "what's love got to do with it?" In this case, fourteen years of labor, working for his slick uncle!

So this was the cultural economy and the historical backdrop in which these scriptures we like to quote were written—not to mention the fact that Solomon, who wrote Proverbs, was "Mr. 700 wives and 300 concubines" himself. Solomon took finding "a good thing" to a *whole-notha-level.*

Another aspect concerning marriage that you had back then, and still find today in some Middle-Eastern countries, is pre-arranged marriages. In these situations, for whatever reason, the parents picked their children's spouses, sometimes years in advance. Imagine that today, ladies. Your dad or mom goes out and finds you a husband, brings him home, and then says, "Y'all go get married. Don't worry about love, you'll learn to do that later!"

Please understand, I'm not suggesting that Proverbs 18:22, is wrong. It's true. But I also wanted you to understand that there was more to consider back in Solomon's day, and there is certainly more to consider today as well. So you can passively sit in a corner with your antennas up, broadcasting, "I'm available," like it's some kind of S.O.S. if you want too. Antennas up or not, sitting there hoping some tall, dark and handsome guy cut to order, is going to just walk up and find you—you are going to be looking crazy and feeling lonely for a long time. Why? Simply because you have overreacted to this one verse!

Chapter 2

IT'S ALRIGHT TO MAKE THE FIRST MOVE

"Making the first move doesn't imply that you are desperate, nor does it make you any less of a lady."

Due to traditional conditioning, many women are often skeptical about making the first move. Consider this, when God created Adam and Eve, He did not tell Adam to go over to where Eve was. He did not push Adam, saying, "Go on over there." But actually, He brought Eve to Adam, that was the first move. Oftentimes we want to put God in a box and say this is the only way He can work. You can't put God in a box.

Moses and Zippora

On one occasion, Moses protected the seven daughters of Jethro by fending off harassing herdsmen and then also fed their sheep. They were so happy that they came home to their daddy Jethro, bragging about Moses, talking about how tough he was, how kind he was, how nice he was, how protective he was, and how he fed their sheep. Jethro said, "Well, where is he? You mean y'all left him?" He told his daughters, "Go get him!" Zippora said parenthetically, "Daddy, you ain't said nothing but a word." It wasn't long before Zippora and Moses were standing at the altar.

Queen Esther

Another Old Testament example that we can learn from is Queen Esther. Esther wasn't passively waiting to be discovered by a knight in shiny armor. However, enlisting herself as a candidate in a national beauty contest was a bold *first move*, and was pivotal in her successful pursuit of Mr. Right.

For an entire year, Esther was preparing herself to get chosen by the man she had her eyes on. Yes, there was some competition, but that's usually the case. There is always someone else that wants the same man you are after, but don't worry about them, just get ready.

During that time, Esther prepared specifically to impress her king and soon-to-be husband. She received the best spa treatments the world has ever known. She spent six months getting oil of myrrh treatments and six months with perfumes and preparations for the beautifying of women. On top of that, her preparation included training in royal protocol and etiquette.

When it was Esther's turn to go in to see the king, she sought wise counsel from the king's chief advisor, and did only what he told her to do and say. The rest is history. Esther's first move paid off big-time—she became the queen of Persia.

I have brought up all these Bible texts and ancient cultural mores for a reason. It's important to understand that we should definitely have a biblical world view. However, sometimes our Christian traditions can get in the way, particularly when it comes to what scriptures are traditionally applied to our relationship experiences today. So this is why I felt that this teaching would be so vital as a source of encouragement and understanding, because many women are losing their grip on "be anxious for nothing," as they keep hitting the snooze button on their biological clocks.

There is an old axiom that says, "the more things change, the more things still stay the same." And when it comes to relationships between men and women, believe it or not, hardly anything has changed. Granted, Solomon may not have had Facebook or Match.com, but word surely got out about his wisdom and his wealth. When it reached the ears of this one fine "sista," her ears and her heart began to tingle. Though Solomon was given supernatural wisdom above any man before him, as we will see, King Solomon wasn't the only one with wisdom. This sista not only had it, she knew how to work it, too. What she did and how she did it worked back then and still works today.

Chapter 3

WHO'S ZOOMIN' WHO?

"First get yourself together, before you starting looking for a man, because while you're checking them out, they are checking you out."

In the mid 1980's, the Queen of Soul, Aretha Franklin had a hit entitled Who's Zoomin' Who. In the context of this song, "zoomin" meant, checkin' somebody out. While the guy thought he was doing all the "checking out," in reality he was the one who had already been checked-out, hence the question "Who's zoomin' who?"

Now granted, the Queen of Soul wasn't

talking about the Queen of Sheba, however, like I said earlier, the more things change, the more they stay the same. Having said that, let's return to the first verse of our text as we examine the dynamics of being "In Pursuit of Mr. Right." Our text reads:

> When the queen of Sheba heard about the fame of Solomon and his relation to the name of the LORD, she came to test him with hard questions.

Point number one: the Queen of Sheba *came looking* for Solomon. If there is one thing that I have learned after many years of marriage, women know how to look for stuff. I mean, if I can't find a pair of socks or a particular shirt, I ask my wife. If she doesn't know where it is, she certainly knows where to look for it. Men are usually baffled by this.

I marvel at my wife as she can go shopping and meticulously find the right item at the right price, get what she wants and save money too. That's a gift. That's why most men go crazy following their wives around in a store. Men are too tunnel-visioned, but women, y'all know how to look for the right stuff. So this is an innate ability that most women have that needs to be engaged, particularly while in pursuit of Mr. Right.

The *Only* One for You?

Many people would tell you that there is only one person in this whole world that will match you, to whom you can be united in holy matrimony. That's a school of thought that may make us get goose pimples and make us say that's real romantic, but think about what it's saying. What that's suggesting is that out of all of the 6.94 billion people in the world, no matter where you live, God is going to somehow someway bring the two of you together, and you will live happily ever after. Now, without sounding like I'm trying to put limits on God, which I am not, I do need to inform you that there is a problem with that popular school of thought. Unfortunately, a whole lot of you have bought into that notion.

That theory, friends, may contribute to the skyrocketing divorce rate. We know that God is anti-divorce, and most Christians that get divorced know that, too. Interestingly, as a pastor,

I have conducted countless counseling sessions with husbands and wives whose marriages are on the rocks. And do you know what a lot of wives' justification for divorce is? They reason that "he wasn't my husband anyway."

So what is the real implication of a statement like that? They are suggesting that the person that they married was not "the one." In essence, they are saying that when they married the "wrong person" and got divorced, that one doesn't count. So on that slippery slope, they marry again, and they find out that the next one isn't "the one" either. What they end up doing is keep on divorcing until they find that one man in the whole world that has been made specifically for them.

If you were all-knowing, you could do that. If you lived forever, you would have time for that. But short of omniscience and immortality, you can't do that! If you keep on doing that, you'll end up like the Samaritan woman that Jesus met at Jacob's Well, who had been married five times, and was "shacking-up" when Jesus confronted her. (I told you, some things don't change.) This isn't how it works! The priority is finding a person who is in the will of God and who has the same goals in life. That's the union God will bless. This is why He says, "Do not be yoked together with unbelievers," (2 Cor. 6:14). Two cannot walk together unless they are in agreement.

You can leave here today and move to New York and find a good man, a person you have something in common with and who has a heart for the Lord. If God connects you, God will bless that union. By the same token, you can change your mind and say, "I'm not going to New York. I'm going to Detroit," or "I'm going to Memphis," and you can have a divine connection where you meet somebody, have something in common with them, are equally yoked, and God can bless that union too.

You are going to mess up thinking that there is only one person out there for you. That's why some women, when they find a man who has absolutely nothing going for himself, a big zero, they won't let him go. They just stalk him—won't let him go because they think there is only one man in the world who can meet their needs. However, this is as wrong as two left shoes.

There are a whole lot of factors that will kill that theory. First of all, don't you know that the federal and state prisons, as well as our county jails, have a large number of our African American men? At last count, there were eight-hundred-forty-six-thousand plus African American men in the United States prison system. You can call yourself waiting on one of them if you want to, but I guarantee that you will be waiting a long time.

Ironically, many of these career inmates, that continuously recidivate, have been married three and four times, and are actually in jail for assaulting or killing their wives. What if the man you have fixated on is really homosexual? Some men are openly effeminate, while others are bisexual, what we call being on the "down-low." You couldn't look at these guys and tell they have homosexual tendencies. They are six-foot-five, tall, dark, and handsome, but they have some secrets. So the issues that Black women have are: a great number of men are incarcerated, others have a serious sexual identity crisis, and numerically, there are more women in the world than men anyway.

In Pursuit of *Mr. Right*

So whoever thinks that "Mack daddy" is the only man in the world for you "cause he's so fine," you make the mistake of not thinking clearly. Your grandmama said, "Don't be no fool, baby girl." Quit ignoring obvious signs, talking about "love will find a way." That kind of foolishness is not love at all, and will *find your way* to the hospital, or *find your way* broke or worse. This is why you don't get stuck on thinking there's only one out there for you. You may only *choose* one, but that doesn't mean that there was *only* one to choose from—there's more than one sweet grape on a vine.

As we go back to our text, let's extract some golden nuggets of ageless truth concerning how the Queen of Sheba found her Mr. Right, King Solomon. There are three important points that need to be emphasized. Point number one, the Queen of Sheba has herself together before she goes looking for her man. How do we know this? I'll say it again, "Queen" of Sheba. That's right. This woman was a queen already. She already had her stuff together. She already had her prominence, her prestige, and her popularity. She already had position, power, and possession. Her reputation already preceded her. She already knew who, what, when, and where she was, and didn't need validation. She was already special.

Chapter 4

THE QUEEN OF SHEBA
(Historical Perspective)

"Never go looking for your half to complete you. One is a whole number."

When considering the Queen of Sheba, many people make the mistake of calling her Queen Sheba, as if Sheba was her name. No, she was the Queen *of* Sheba. According to Strong's Hebrew Dictionary, the name Sheba is in reference to "the name of three early progenitors of tribes and of an Ethiopian district." So whatever her real name was, it isn't important, because her title speaks for itself. This stunning sista was the

Queen of Ethiopia.

At this point, please engage me as I digress briefly. The Ethiopia of today is not the same as the ancient region called Ethiopia in the Queen of Sheba's day. The territory was called Nubia, which today would encompass the regions of southern Egypt and the Republic of Sudan. There is some interesting history between Ethiopia and the Jews. For example, Moses married an Ethiopian woman (Num. 12:1), and though the Bible doesn't mention it, if Moses had children with her, they would have been Black. Why do I say this? Because in Jeremiah 13:23, the passage asks the rhetorical question, "Can the Ethiopian change his skin?" Which is an obvious reference to Ethiopians' distinctively dark complexion.

The Jewish historian, Josephus, speaks of the Queen of Sheba as being the Queen of Egypt and Ethiopia (Jos. Antiq. VIII. 6). However, one of the most interesting accounts concerning Solomon and the Queen of Sheba is found in the Ethiopian "Kebre Negast," the ancient book that chronicles Ethiopia's history. Of its many accounts, the Kebre Negast records the story of Solomon and the Queen of Sheba. They had a son between them by the name of Menelik, who would become the first Emperor of Ethiopia. He was instrumental in bringing Judaism to Ethiopia and started a line of Ethiopian Jews that has lasted to this day.

We see evidence of this in the book of Acts. In chapter 8, we find an Ethiopian eunuch in Gaza, who was the treasurer of Candace, the Queen of the Ethiopians. The eunuch was reading Isaiah 53. When Philip the evangelist met up with him in Gaza, Philip preached Christ to him and the eunuch was baptized and converted from Judaism to Christianity. This high ranking Ethiopian official took the Gospel back to Ethiopia (Africa) decades before Paul stepped foot in Europe, where he converted Lydia in Thyatira. It is inspiring to know that God blessed the Ethiopians through a love affair that goes all the way back to the relationship between Solomon and the Queen of Sheba.

The Queen of Sheba
(Model for Today's Progressive Women)

Now I have said all of this to you sista's out there to encourage you. We can learn a lot from our own kind. She's a queen looking for a king, and since she's a queen, she already has what Solomon has. Solomon has a caravan, she has a caravan. Solomon has a posse, she has a posse. Solomon has servants. She says, "I've got servants." Solomon has a castle, she has a castle. Solomon has cash, she has her own cash.

So what can we learn from this? We can learn that it is not necessary for you to find a man to help you get yourself together. The Queen of Sheba had herself together *before* she went looking for a man. Unfortunately, we talk about, "I'm looking for my better half." No, you shouldn't be looking for no other half, because you should be whole already. If I'm together and I'm whole, and he's together and he's whole, then our joy shall be doubled.

Some of you may be saying, "all this is fine if you're privileged like the Queen of Sheba. I work at a bank, or a grocery store. I'm not a queen." But I beg to differ with you, because you are one of the daughters of Christ, and the scripture declares that we are children of the Most High and have royal connections everywhere. 1 Peter 2:9 says you are "a chosen generation, a royal priesthood." See there, you are special. And this is something you should look in the mirror every morning and say to yourself: "I'm special."

Proverbs 18:21 says that life and death are in the power of the tongue. That's why you need to hear yourself saying, "I'm special. I'm a child of the King and I am of royal lineage." In Romans 10:17, the Bible also says faith comes by hearing. This is why the world has picked up on this concept and spends billions of dollars in marketing, so you can hear their message and buy their products. You need to stop saying, "But I've got low self esteem." Start saying, "I'm special." You see, it's all in knowing who you really are. Romans 8:17 says, "we are heirs of God and joint heirs with Christ."

So using the Queen of Sheba as our model for dating, one of the first things we can glean from her dealings with King Solomon is that if you are going to be successful in your pursuit of a man, you have to bring something to the table. She came as a queen, and not only did she have some attributes and assets, but akin to that, according to verses 13 and 14, she left as a queen. When you begin a relationship, when you get involved with people, the same dignity you brought to the relationship is the same dignity you should still have when you leave. Never be willing to compromise yourself.

Stop violating your own conscience. At the end of the day, you are the one who has to be able to live with yourself. When you lie down at night, you don't want to toss and turn in condemnation because you have compromised. The consequences of compromise are not worth it. You shouldn't come into a relationship as a queen and leave as a queer. You shouldn't come into a relationship as a princess and leave as a prostitute. You shouldn't come in with royalty and resources, and leave with rags.

Chapter 5

NEVER ABANDON YOUR SUPPORT SYSTEM

"Never allow anyone to cause you to sabotage the relationships and the support systems that helped develop you into the woman that you are."

In the second verse of our text, we learn a very important concept. Put simply, when looking for your man, *never leave your support system behind.* When the Queen of Sheba arrived, she had her posse with her, and when she returned to Ethiopia, she left with her posse. She arrived with an entourage, and she went back to Africa with an entourage. In order to come with something and leave later with something, that means you had to maintain it while you were there.

There's a tendency nowadays that people want to clip your connection to your support system. Many of you attend wonderful churches. If you go to Greater St. John Bible Church, you have a great support system spiritually, because you will get the Word taught to you. It's a place where your life can be developed. Jesus said, "I have come to give you life, and life more abundantly. That's what you want, the more abundant life."

The way you achieve that "more abundant life" is through the impartation of the Holy Spirit and through the Word of God. This is why being grounded and rooted is so important. You have to be still long enough to get watered and nourished so God can give you the increase. This is why you should be under good and sound teaching. It's all a part of your support system.

Also, there are other forms of support that play a vital role in our day-to-day walk with the Lord. I don't care who you are, you will experience a time or a season when you will need some assistance. No one is an island unto themselves.

In Pursuit of *Mr. Right*

We all need help sometimes. This is why we have missionaries who visit you when you are sick and care for you when you are going through situations, and pray for you when you have tragedies, and celebrate with you when you have victories. This is all part of your great support system! Don't let anybody take that from you.

Some of you have great parents who have laid it all on the line for you, have sacrificed for you, who gave everything, their sweat and blood for you. Don't you let no joker cut you off from your family support system. You have friends who love you. You have friends who have been better to you than your own relatives; friends who have been with you through thick and thin. Don't you let anybody cut you off from your friends. Some of you have mentors, big brothers or big sisters, a father-figure, or a peer-mentor, who look after you and hold you accountable. Don't let anybody disconnect you from that.

Yes, that's right. We need both friends and mentors, but in many cases, mentors are better than friends. A friend loves you like you are, but a mentor loves you too much to leave you like you are. A friend says, "You are my dog. You are my homey. I love you and we are going to be together through thick and thin." A mentor says, "I love you, but come on up. You can do better than this. I see greatness inside of you. Step on up a little higher."

All these different types and levels of relationships are very important. That's why you shouldn't get so desperate that you let people cut you off from your support system. Some guys are very dominating and controlling, and will even try to choose your friends. "You stay away from her. I can see through her," they insist. Your response should be, "No, we were friends long before I met you." Men with controlling personalities will even start to alienate you from your family.

Now, granted you should not be running back and forth to your mama and daddy after every encounter or conversation with your man, but no one has any business telling you that you can't talk to your family members. So be aware and be careful to avoid a man, or anyone, who tries to destroy your support system and alienate you from your family. This is a behavior that does not get better with time. If it's bad in the beginning, it will get worse later. If you have to say, "Wait a minute, this is my family, who loved me long before I ever met you," more than once, then they're not getting the message, and you should be getting out of there. Behaviors like that are a serious red flag to proceed no further.

The first area subject to being sabotaged is one's spiritual support system. You probably can't see it every Sunday or during mid-week Bible class. For example, on Sunday mornings, the seat that was usually occupied by sister-so-and-so is now noticeably empty. Or you may also notice how chairs being placed in the aisles are no longer needed. Do you know what happened to these sisters? They were kidnapped from church. You can always tell when some folks have a new "boo."

Yes indeed, you can certainly tell when somebody has a new man. You can tell when somebody is dating. As long as they don't have anybody, they are tearing the door off the hinges to get into church. But when they get somebody, you can't catch up with them. It's no mystery. It wasn't a close encounter of the third kind; it was a too close encounter of the *man* kind. That's what I mean when I say kidnapped.

Another issue is that too many women want to put the cart ahead of the horse in a relationship. The Queen of Sheba went to *meet* King Solomon, not to *marry* him. We have too many folks who want to put the cart before the horse. I'm just basically trying to tell you to stop thinking that every man you meet is the man you are going to marry. Whenever you do that, there is a palpable level of desperation that you bring to the table. All the guy said was, "I just thought I would call because I had tickets to see Chris Tucker. Or I just thought I would call you because I had tickets to a Bulls' game. I just thought I would call you because I wanted to go to Red Lobster."

It was a lunch date, movie date, mall date, comedy show date, not a proposal date. Some of you are so desperate; you can't get past a hamburger before you start interviewing the guy for marriage. Take some sound advice, and slow down, sister, slow down. You have to meet the man before you marry him.

Chapter 6

THE VALUE OF A GOOD REPUTATION

"Guard your reputation at all cost and pay significant attention to the reputation of your prospective partner."

Another very important precept that we can extract from verse one of our thematic text, is that it was Solomon's reputation that captured the Queen of Sheba's interest.

> When the queen of Sheba heard about the fame of Solomon and his relation to the name of the LORD, she came to test him with hard questions.

Have you ever heard the saying, "your reputation precedes you?" Well, it does. Word gets out and spreads quickly about people. Long before Marvin Gaye made his song, "Heard it Through the Grapevine," the grapevine was already the hotline. So, centuries before the Internet and Facebook, it didn't take long for a reputation to spread.

When I was in high school, I was on the track team, where I ran cross-country. I will admit it, I was quite proud of myself because I knew I could either sprint or run long distance. However, my grandmama said to me one day, "I don't care how fast you run, you can never outrun your own reputation." Your reputation is faster than you and will beat you to a place. You can't outrun your reputation.

The Queen of Sheba heard about King Solomon, and after considering all of what she had been hearing, the hooks were in her and she got interested—real interested. The word of Solomon's reputation, his accomplishments, and his achievements had traveled all the way to the motherland Africa, beyond the rivers of Ethiopia. This is why you must guard your reputation. Proverbs 22:1 says: "A good name is more desirable than great riches; to be esteemed is better than silver or gold." This is why being upright and honest is so important. Do not cheat anyone, because a good name is worth more than the few dollars you connived to obtain.

Don't compromise your values and morals that you've been taught by your parents, pastors, teachers, and mentors, because a good name is more desirable than great wealth, and to be esteemed is better than money. This is especially important for you women. Many of you know how it feels the next morning after you have given up the goodies too soon. After the thrill is gone, so is the guy. Now all you have left is the emptiness you feel on the inside. You're not fulfilled, you feel cheap, especially after the word gets out that you sleep around. That's a hard reputation to live down.

In Acts chapter 6, we learn that the Apostles chose deacons to help them operate and manage the ministry. What was their priority when they were looking for people? They didn't look for MBA's or accountants. They weren't looking for people who were managers. Those types of qualifications were not the criteria they were looking for. They went to find some men of honest report, men of character, men of good reputation. That's who they placed over the business of the church.

So now, ask yourself this question: what are they saying about the man in whom I have interest? What are people whose opinions count saying about him? Not individuals who don't like him or people who hate him. I'm speaking of people who have credibility when they speak. What are his associates saying about him? What are his homies saying about him? What are his peers saying about him? And in particular, what is his family saying about him? Let me tell you something, and you'd better hear.

I once heard Oprah Winfrey quoting Dr. Maya Angelou, saying, "whatever a person says they are, believe them. If he says 'I'm a player,' then believe him. And if his own mother says, 'he ain't no good,' believe her; that fellow ain't no good." Here is where a lot of women drop the ball. They do not want to believe what they are seeing and hearing. They want to ignore the obvious because somehow they believe that love will find the way, or that they can change somebody. You simply cannot make a shoe that is too small fit. No matter how good that pair of shoes look, no matter how well it goes with your outfit, a shoe that's too small will only cause you pain.

Chapter 7

CHALLENGE HIS WISDOM

"Asking the right questions at the right time will help you determine whether a man is a pretender or a contender."

The Queen of Sheba heard all the reports. She heard about King Solomon's opulent palace and the enormity of his wealth. She heard about his work, and his wisdom, so now she was coming to witness all this for herself. Even more importantly, she came to test the accuracy of all she had heard, and the best way to do that, was to challenge his wisdom.

There are three points I want to share with you. Number one, challenge his wisdom. The

Queen of Sheba came a long way to ask Solomon some hard questions. Once you meet a person and you want to elevate in the relationship, you have to ask some hard questions. You can't be throwing softball questions. You have to throw some hardball questions, knowing that he'll either hit a home run, or strike out.

When I was growing up, we used to play Piggy in the park or in the backyard. We'd take the softball and we'd throw a slow pitch. Your friend might tell you, "Put it down the middle." So you'd just take your time and give a slow pitch. You would intentionally make it real easy for them to hit.

Once you begin a relationship, things can become intense very quickly. That is why you must approach dating seriously—not like slow-pitch-Piggy. Your approach should be like playing hardball in the major leagues. Sometimes you watch those baseball players waiting for that hundred-mile-an-hour ball to come, and the pitcher is saying, "I'm going to knock him off his feet." Ask the hardball questions that will make him back up off that plate.

In Pursuit of *Mr. Right*

What is an example of those Piggy-pitches? Questions like, What's your favorite color? What's your Zodiac sign? What high school did you attend? Or what team did you support? "I'm a Westinghouse Warrior." "I'm a Marshall Commando." "I'm a Steinmetz High Silver Streak." Okay, I get it! This type of light conversation is all right when you are just reminiscing or getting together to have some fun. However, when you are trying to elevate your life to another dimension, and are interested in a committed relationship, you have to ask pointed questions like: "Are you a Christian?" "Do you go to church?" "How often do you go to church?" Some people are claiming church membership but they only attend once a year.

If he comes back and says, "Yeah, I go to church," don't stop there. Hit him with another series of fastballs. Ask him, "Where is your church? What's the pastor's name?" "What's your favorite scripture?" And just in case he remembers a scripture from Sunday school back when he was in kindergarten, ask him: "Where's that scripture found?" If he responds with something like, "it's somewhere in the book of *palms*," you'll know what's *really* going on!

However, even if he comes up with the right answers for those questions, the game is not over yet. That was just the first inning. Now this is the start of another inning. Start off with a low and inside fast ball pitch that's going to make him back up a little. "Where do you work? What do you do? Do you pay your bills? What's your credit score?" If he's doing well so far, now is not the time to let up. Throw him some curve balls. "Are you a child molester? Is your name on that list?" Have you ever been to jail?" (You certainly don't want any switch hitters!)

If he hasn't started sweating by now, remember the game is not over yet; there still are some innings left. This time, aim for the head and see if you can make him duck. Remember he told you he was a Christian. Ask him, "Are you married? What are your views on shacking up? Are you in a serious relationship now?" Ask the hard questions. "Do you have any children? Do you pay your child support?"

You don't have to nail him like a prosecuting attorney. However, you should be tactful, sweet, and cordial. You can say, "This is a real nice car that you're driving, but whose is it? Is it a loner or a lease?" (You do know that a guy will borrow a car to make a good impression on a new girl friend, don't you?) Continue with the tough questions. "Do you live with your mama, or does your mama live with you?" (There really is a difference you know.) It's really important to ask questions like these.

Some of you reading this book may be thinking, my God, do I really have to ask all these questions? The simple answer is—you'd better. Asking the tough questions in the beginning will spare you from all the hard answers in the end. The fact is, whether you ask these questions or not, you will be getting the answers later. When the tough questions are asked, won't change any of the facts. But they will help expose problems before it's too late. So even if you are not into sports, you can still be good at playing hardball.

Confirm His Wealth

The second point is, after the Queen of Sheba challenged Solomon's wisdom, she then confirmed his wealth. "I heard about it. They told me about it. I got the report, but I came to see it.

I want to lay my eyes on it myself." Verses 4 and 5 say:

> When the queen of Sheba saw all the wisdom of Solomon and the palace he had built *[not his mama's house]*, the food on his table, the seating of his officials, the attending servants in their robes, his cupbearers, and the burnt offerings he made at the temple of the LORD *[he put his own money in church; he didn't just attach his name on his old lady's envelope; some men don't ever put any money in church, they just say, "Put my name on the envelope, baby."]*, she was overwhelmed. (emphasis mine)

She saw it herself. She saw economic development. She saw community development. She was blown away, overwhelmed, speechless, humbled. You had better confirm a person's wealth when you are trying to date them or when you're interested or when you're pursuing them. Confirm their wealth, especially those of you who are contemplating getting married or having a serious relationship that leads to marriage. The number one cause of divorce in America is money. There are some people who survive a whole lot of other issues and drama and hang in there, but when you mess with their money, they say, "I'm out of here."

She saw how much he gave to God. Don't let a guy fool you into thinking that he loves God if he doesn't give God something. Don't let a guy tell you, "I love the Lord. I am very faithful to Him and His calling and His Kingdom," but he's not giving God anything. He's full of crap. That's just Ira Acree's way of paraphrasing the scripture that says where your treasure lies, there will your heart be also.

You can tell what's significant in a man's life by how he spends his money. Don't you ever forget that the truth of the matter is, if he says he loves God and won't give God something, what makes you think that if he says he loves you, he will give you something? You can't compete with God, I don't care how good you think you are. You can't compare with God. You can't ever be as good to him as God has been. You have never saved his soul. You didn't cause him to wake up in the morning. You've never saved him from the Devil's grasp or from hell's fiery furnace. Don't ever forget this principle: giving to God is more about faith than finance. It's more about the attitude than the amount. If you believe and your heart is right, you wouldn't dare try to rob God of the tithe that already belongs to Him.

Solomon had blown this girl's mind. She said, "I was over in Africa. I heard about your wisdom. I heard about your wealth. I heard about your work. Therefore, I came to see all this for myself. And now that I'm here, I want you to know that they really didn't do you justice. You are better than they said you are. The half has not been told." What a man, what a man, what a mighty good man.

Check Out His Work

In our final point, verse 7 says:

> But I did not believe these things until I came and saw with my own eyes. Indeed, not even half was told me; in wisdom and wealth you have far exceeded the report I heard.

As we can see from the above passage, the

In Pursuit of *Mr. Right*

Queen of Sheba did not believe what she had been hearing about Solomon. How many times have we all been disappointed by inflated, exaggerated, embellished, blown-up accounts of how someone is or isn't? We have all been taken in by the deceptiveness of misleading accounts. We have all experienced being misguided by the rumor mill.

Can you imagine what the Queen of Sheba must have heard? "Girl, did you hear about the way King Solomon was able to determine who was the true mother of a baby that two women claimed was theirs? By ordering that the baby be cut in half and split between the two women! However, the real mother stepped up and said, "No! Let the other woman have the baby." Solomon knew that only the real mother would have given the baby up to preserve its life, and that's how he was able to determine the truth."

The Queen of Sheba might have said, "hmmm, can anyone truly be that wise?" Then I'm sure she heard that Solomon's temple was simply breathtaking and opulent, with unparalleled architecture and dressed with the finest marble, ivory, silver, and gold. I'm sure she heard, "You've got to see it. There is nothing in the world like it." The Queen of Sheba might have said, "Yeah, I hear you talking, but I'm not going to believe it until I see it for myself."

Even though the Queen heard all of this, but she had to check out his work for herself. Translated into today's vernacular, "I see you in this uniform, but do you have a job? I see you wearing this I.D. badge but you may not have turned it in when you lost your job!" I know it's a recession and all of that, so you have to be really honest; there are a lot of men not working. But if your man isn't working, he ought to at least be willing to work. He ought to have a work ethic.

I have made my share of mistakes being a pastor, and I'm sure I'll make more. But there's one mistake I will never make again. I will never marry a couple where the man doesn't work, again. Not working *before* you get married usually translates into; I don't have to work *once* I get married. If that is your situation, just go ahead and join another church because I'm not going to be a contributor to destroying your life. If he doesn't work, it is a very strong indication that the marriage is not going to work either.

That's why you should have the same attitude as Cuba Gooding, Jr. had in the film *Jerry Maguire* when he said his now famous mantra, "Show me the money." You want to see the money he earns from a respectable job. I emphasize *respectable* job because you want to know where the money is coming from. If your man is driving a nice car, has lots of cash, a nice place to live, but doesn't have a regular job or own a legitimate business, then something is wrong with that.

Chapter 8

LADIES SAVE YOUR SPICES!

"Don't go so fast with the goodies! Easy women rarely get chosen by kings."

In verse 10 of our thematic text we find the next point that I would like to expand upon. The verse says:

> And she gave the king 120 talents of gold, large quantities of spices, and precious stones...

I know some of you are saying, "Rev., you were doing fine till you got to this verse! I'm not giving a man my hard earned money." "You were just saying that he needs to have his own." Well before you have a conniption, I urge you not to get me wrong or misinterpret this verse. However, there are a lot of women out there that do have a "that's why I take care of my man" mentality. But that's not what I am emphasizing here. To have a meaningful relationship is not about you being a "sugar-mama" and taking care of "pretty boy" Tony.

In the context and economy of this ancient text, whenever a king came to meet with another king, the visiting king, or in this case a queen, always brought gifts. The amount or magnitude of the gift was a reflection of honor and respect that the visiting king was bestowing upon the host king. Had the Queen of Sheba shown up with a pair of Nikes, that would not have gone over very well and would have suggested a low impression of King Solomon. Even to this day, when heads of state visit one another, they always exchange gifts, as do the first ladies.

Today this gift exchange between heads of state is merely symbolic. But back in those days, they gave gifts of tremendous substance, which is one of the reasons why Solomon was so rich. Proverbs 18:16, says: "A gift opens the way and ushers the giver into the presence of the great." In other words, when you show honor and respect, you should expect honor and respect in return.

Even though the Queen of Sheba gave tremendously to Solomon, King Solomon also gave back to the queen. The fact of the matter is that the Queen of Sheba actually left with more than she came with. You see, a wise king would not let the visitor be more generous or gracious then he. In a real relationship, there is the dynamic of giving and reciprocation. A solid relationship is not one-sided—it goes both ways. It's almost a who-out-gave-who situation. There has to be some reciprocity involved.

Returning back to our text, verse 2 says:

> She came to Jerusalem with a very great retinue, with camels that bore spices, very much gold, and precious stones; and when she came to Solomon, she spoke with him about all that was in her heart.

In this verse, we can extract some romantic

details. The queen brought spices and told the king all that was in her heart. As we stated earlier, there are legends, such as those found in the Kebre Negast, that say the Queen of Sheba and Solomon got married. You know she came a long way. She came all the way from Africa. But in her desperation, on her journey, even with difficulties, she kept her spices for Solomon. There were men who were with her, but they didn't get her spices.

Surely there were other kings and other kingdoms that she as a head of state undoubtedly encountered. She kept men with her, who would have done anything she told them to do, but they didn't get her spices because she saved them for her king. I say this from my heart. That's what makes me uncomfortable as a pastor, when I see all these young adult women in our church. I plead to you today, don't give away your spices. I know I'm old-school; I'm over forty. But please don't give away your spices, so you will have some spices to give to your king, when you meet him. And you still want your spices to be good. To further illustrate this point, let me borrow from the Gospels, where Jesus said,

In Pursuit of *Mr. Right*

> "...if the salt loses its saltiness, how can it be made salty again? It is no longer good for anything, except to be thrown out and trampled underfoot.
>
> Matthew 5:13

Savor your seasoning. Cherish your spices, because once they lose their preciousness, men will only despise them and trample them under foot. Do you want your spices trampled on? If you allow your spices to be trampled on, that makes you a tramp. A tramp is a woman who allows men to misuse and abuse her. So that should never be you, because you are a queen.

Now I do understand that we were not all born saved, and that we all have some shame in our past. But now in Christ, you are a new creation, and you are of a royal priesthood. Your daddy is the King of kings, and the Lord of lords, who has paid all your sin debt. You are free to be the queen that God called you to be.

You bring many gifts to a relationship. Like the Queen of Sheba, you bring a caravan of precious spices and fragrant ointments. Your jewels are costly, and your gold and silver shine bright with the light of God's love. Your pearls are too expensive to be thrown before swine, who cannot appreciate their uniqueness and value. You are nobody's tramp to be trampled upon. You are only to be respected, cherished, and loved.

The Princess and the Frog

There is a movie called *The Princess and the Frog*. I like this Disney production because it features the first African American princess in that studio's history. The critics called it a great romantic comedy. Unfortunately, it perpetuates an old fairytale mentality to a new generation of young girls—that a frog is a prince in disguise.

However, here is a tidbit of wisdom from the book of Acree: if it's green like a frog, and croaks like a frog, and leaps like a frog—it's a frog! You don't have to pray about it. You don't have to fast about it. You don't have to call and worry me about it. He's a frog! And I don't care how many times you kiss him, he ain't gonna change into a prince! So my advice to you is, stop kissing frogs!

Some time ago, there was a hilarious credit

card commercial that aired on television featuring a beautiful princess. She had her stuff together. She had her crown, she had all her royal attire. However, she's a lonely princess and here comes a frog. She kisses this frog, and instead of it becoming a prince, the frog turns into a weasel. She kisses the weasel, but instead of the weasel becoming a prince, the weasel turns into a buzzard.

She goes back "one-more-again." She kisses the buzzard, and instead of the buzzard turning into a prince, the buzzard turns into a skunk. She kisses the skunk, but instead of the skunk turning into a prince, the skunk turns into a monkey. She kisses the monkey, but instead of the monkey turning into a prince, he turns into this half-man half-jackass. She throws up her hands and runs. "Hey, hey" says the half-man half-jackass. "Come on back. You're just one more kiss away from your prince!"

You get the point. Sisters, let me ask you a question. How many weasels are you going to kiss? How many buzzards are you going to kiss? How many monkeys are you going to kiss? How many skunks are you going to kiss? How many half-men and half you-know-whats are you going to kiss? How many half-asses are you going to kiss trying to turn them into a prince?

Your kiss ain't that tough and it can't turn a jackass into a prince. Your kiss can't turn a weasel who won't work into a prince. Your kiss won't turn a skunk who won't serve the Lord into a prince, and your kiss certainly won't turn a frog who likes to hop from relationship to relationship into a prince. Whatever that joker was before you kissed him, that's exactly what he is going to be after you kiss him. And even if you compromise and are intimate with him, he'll be the same weasel after you're done, and you'll be the same fool for thinking you could change him in the first place.

Chapter 9

Final Words

"Before you begin your pursuit of Mr. Right, make sure you have a personal relationship with the ultimate Mr. Right, Jesus Christ Himself. A foundation built upon Him will sustain your relationship—there's nobody greater."

In the Bible, we find that the marital relationship is used metaphorically, in what are referred to as types and shadows. For example, in the book of Song of Songs or as the King James translates it, Song of Solomon, we find an intense love affair between Solomon and his "dark" and lovely bride. Though it is debatable, many have likened the relationship depicted here to a type of Christ and the Church.

On the other end of the spectrum, we have the prophet Hosea, who weds a prostitute named Gomer. Here in poignant prophetic portrayal, the relationship between Jehovah and His bride, the adulterous nation of Israel, is played out for all to see. Here we learn that God's willingness to love is more powerful than Israel's propensity to be unfaithful. All these spiritual and moral dynamics are played out through Hosea's marriage to Gomer. And in Jeremiah, once again God cries out to His people when He says: "Turn, O backsliding children, saith the LORD; for I am married unto you," (Jer. 3:14 KJV).

Whether actual or symbolic, we can see that the Bible has much to say about marriage. Whether it is the day-to-day relationship between a husband and a wife, or whether it's a metaphor used to depict contrast and conflicts of an intimate relationship between God and His people, marriage is a very serious subject. Since marriage is a direct reflection of God's relationship with His people, this is also why I believe the institution of marriage is under such intense attack by the enemy.

Therefore, of all these practical principles

we have covered in this book, there is something that must remain at the forefront in all we do: there must be a divine connection—and Jesus is that divine connection. Like the gospel music hit "Nobody Greater," by VaShawn Mitchell says, "I searched all over, couldn't find nobody...Nobody greater than you." Since there is nobody greater, Jesus then is the greatest example of how true love and marriage relationship should be. As a matter of fact, Adam becoming one flesh with Eve was actually a foreshadowing or a type of Christ and His bride, the Church.

In Ephesians 5, Paul tells us:

> After all, no one ever hated their own body, but they feed and care for their body, just as Christ does the church—for we are members of his body... "and the two will become one flesh." This is a profound mystery—but I am talking about Christ and the church.

What we see here is only a glimpse of the greatness of the Lord, the divine husbandman. We should take comfort in knowing that the Church is Christ's bride—flesh of His flesh and bone of His bone. The Church is involved in a divine love affair with God Himself. The following scripture gives us a glimpse of the divine pageantry of heaven's greatest wedding ceremony:

> Let us be glad and rejoice, and give honour to him: for the marriage of the Lamb is come, and his wife hath made herself ready. And to her was granted that she should be arrayed in fine linen, clean and white: for the fine linen is the righteousness of saints. And he saith unto me, Write, Blessed are they which are called unto the marriage supper of the Lamb. And he saith unto me, These are the true sayings of God.
> Revelation 19:7-9 KJV

So if the ultimate reality of marriage is patterned after Christ and the Church, then the ultimate Mr. Right is Jesus Christ Himself. He is the divine husbandman. Since there is nobody greater, we all should first be in pursuit of the ultimate Mr. Right, Jesus Christ, the righteousness of God. With this in mind, let all the women who desire to be married be led by the heavenly

In Pursuit of *Mr. Right*

Mr. Right, before you start off "*in pursuit of Mr. Right*" down here on earth.

The End

Another Exciting Title from Pastor Ira J. Acree

ISBN 978-0-9831317-0-0

The Man in the Mirror is not your typical collection of mundane messages. These inspiring messages emanates out from the heart of Reverend Ira J. Acree, one of Chicago's most dynamic preachers and visionary religious leaders. Reverend Acree masterfully incorporates the gospel message of faith and hope within a contemporary context that is relevant for today's political and economic environment. His sermonic content is informative yet humorous while maintaining homiletic excellence. No matter what denomination, church affiliation, political or economic status, Reverend Acree's thought provoking messages are guaranteed to ignite the transformation power necessary to change the world one Christian at a time.

In Pursuit of Mr. Right, can be purchased through bookstores eveywhere or through Amazon.com, Barnes and Noble.com, and SpringArbor. Availible in eBook too!

Life To Legacy

Let us bring your story to life! With Life to Legacy, we offer the following publishing services: Manuscript development, editing and transcription services, ghostwriting, cover design, copyright services, ISBN assignment, worldwide distribution and eBooks. You maintain control over your project because we are here to serve you.

Even if you do not have a manuscript, we can ghostwrite your story for you from audio recordings and even legible handwritten documents.

We also specialize in family history books, so you can leave a written legacy for your children, grandchildren and others. You put your story in our hands, and we'll bring it to literary life!

Please visit our website:
www.Life2legacy.com, or call us at
877-267-7477
You can also email us at:
Life2legacybooks@att.net

www.ingramcontent.com/pod-product-compliance
Lightning Source LLC
Chambersburg PA
CBHW031213090426
42736CB00009B/901